30 VICTORY LESSONS

FOR TEENS
LESSONS EVERY TEEN NEEDS TO BE VICTORIOUS

CHARLETTE THE CHALLENGER

COPYRIGHT © 2020 BY CHARLETTE THE CHALLENGER

All rights reserved.

ISBN: ISBN-978-1-7338829-0-3

All rights reserved. Non-commercial interests may reproduce portions of this book without the express written permission of the author, provided the text does not exceed 500 words. When reproducing text from this book, include the following credit line: **"30 Victory Lesson for Teens. Used by permission."**

Commercial interests: No part of this publication may be reproduced in any form, stored in a retrieval system, or transmitted in any form by any means - electronic, photocopy, recording, or otherwise - without prior written permission of the publisher, except as provided by the United States of America copyright law.

30 VICTORY LESSONS

FOR TEENS
LESSONS EVERY TEEN NEEDS TO BE VICTORIOUS

THIS BOOK BELONGS TO:

_____

GIVEN TO ON:

_____

DEDICATION

This book is dedicated to my little cousin Byron'Nisha. Whenever I came around you always made sure I stayed on course of doing what I said I would do.

Also, to the graduating class of 2020. I know you have many lessons to share that I have never experienced. I hope you can enjoy the lessons in this book.

CONTENTS

INTRO 1

LESSON NUMBER ONE: "Be Quick To Listen And Slow To Speak." 3

LESSON NUMBER TWO: "Breathe! It Will Be Okay." 6

LESSON NUMBER THREE: "Mistakes Are Blessings!" 9

LESSON NUMBER FOUR: "Growing Never Stops?" 12

LESSON NUMBER FIVE: "Lifting Yourself Up Vs. Beating Yourself" 15

LESSON NUMBER SIX: "Every Decision Count!" 19

LESSON NUMBER 7: "Everyone Has An Opinion!" 22

LESSON NUMBER EIGHT: "Money Is A Tool" 25

LESSON NUMBER NINE: "Guide Your Mind" 28

LESSON NUMBER TEN: "If You Do Not Know Something You Can Find The Answer" 32

LESSON NUMBER ELEVEN: "Peace In Your Mind Is Better" 35

LESSON NUMBER TWELVE: "Love Others As Yourself" 38

LESSON NUMBER THIRTEEN: "Excellence Is A Habit!" 41

LESSON NUMBER FOURTEEN: "Consistence Is Key" 44

LESSON NUMBER FIFTEEN: "Be" 47

LESSON NUMBER SIXTEEN: "Imagine Your Greatness" 50

LESSON NUMBER SEVENTEEN: "Be Bold And Courageous!" 53

LESSON NUMBER EIGHTEEN: "Giving Is One Of The Greatest Rewards" 56

LESSON NUMBER NINETEEN: "You Have To Wanna Change" 59

LESSON NUMBER TWENTY: "Believing In Yourself" 62

LESSON NUMBER TWENTY-ONE: "Success Is Not Given It Is Earned!" 65

LESSON NUMBER TWENTY-TWO: "Quiet Time Is The Best Time!" 68

"BE QUICK TO LISTEN AND SLOW TO SPEAK."

LESSON NUMBER TWENTY-THREE: "Giving Thanks In Every Situation" 71

LESSON NUMBER TWENTY-FOUR: "It's Okay To Say No" 74

LESSON NUMBER TWENTY-FIVE: "Birds Of A Feather Flock Together" 77

LESSON NUMBER TWENTY-SIX: "Victory Is Already Yours" 80

LESSON NUMBER TWENTY-SEVEN: "Don't Settle" 83

LESSON NUMBER TWENTY-EIGHT: "Get Clarity" 86

LESSON TWENTY-NINE: "Get Committed" 89

LESSON NUMBER THIRTY: "Get Confident" 92

VICTORIOUS CONTRACT 95

INTRO

Hi! This book is being written so I can talk with you! Yes You! I want to talk to you about all the things I wish I had known when I was growing up. The things that I worried about so much then, that now, when looking back was not that big of a deal. I want to share with you what I've learned to stay calm in certain situation, however when I was younger I would have flipped all the way out. Also, lesson that I just wished I had known prior to facing them. I am going to share with you a little bit about me and then I will give you 30 Victory Lessons that I have learned thus far.

  I am currently 34 and it is 2020. I'll be 35 in August of this year. I am actually excited about turning 35. I have my own business, an online tv show, and I love promoting other Authors, Non-Profit leaders and creative entrepreneurs. I am also a mother as of today of a 17, 16, and 12-years old young men. Cameron, Emmanuel, and Leslie Jr are the Superstars in my life. I've learned that no matter what happens they will always be my sons and I will always be their mother. My passion to work with you came from being a teenage mother. My junior year I had my first son. Then my senior year, I graduate six months pregnant with my second son. By the time I was Twenty-one I was giving birth to my Third son by the third father. I know what you're thinking… You probably thinking: "What was you thinking?" My answer would be: "I wasn't." I mean, I really did not have a plan. I did not have a direction for my life. I just was existing enjoying life. From parties to being body slammed to the concrete. From being on my kitchen floor with a knife to my throat to having no place to live for me and my children.

"BE QUICK TO LISTEN AND SLOW TO SPEAK."

This was all before the age of 22. Whoa!!! Hold up! Something had to change, I thought. After having life sucked out of me, I sat down and started thinking of a plan for the direction of my life. I asked GOD to lead me in the direction I should go. The change did not happen overnight.

Well that was me fourteen years ago and a lot has changed since then. I have been on a mission to share with many people how to rewrite the script of their life. Not only do I share, but I have a space were many other people from all walks of life share their Victorious stories on the platform that I host such as Victory TV and Victory Events. I enjoy what I do! However, it hasn't been easy. I have finally gotten to a peaceful calm place in my life where I am super high! Not marijuana high either! It's a high to where I have love, power, and a sound mind! It's at the point to where I enjoy Imagining what the future holds for every life that I touch. So here goes! It's your turn. Life is just beginning for you. Here are some things that I would like to tell you!

LESSON NUMBER ONE

"BE QUICK TO LISTEN AND SLOW TO SPEAK."

If I could tell you one of the key ingredients that I learned early in my adult years it was **"BE QUICK TO LISTEN AND SLOW TO SPEAK."**

I can remember at the age of twenty-two sitting down talking with my mom asking her "How did you do it? All the things that I put you through, how were you able to deal with it?" I remember her answer being short and simple with a smirk smile saying, "Girl I had to do what I had to do, what are you talking about?" I was being serious, but she said as if it was a breeze raising 4 kids in a single parent home. At this time my sons was 6, 5, and 1. I was having flashbacks from all the things my mom told me as a youth in my teenage years. Mostly everything she said came true.

It was at this moment I realized that she had lived longer than I had with way more knowledge just by her twenty years more of being on plant earth longer than me. I apologize to her for all the things I put her through. Never once I thought life was hard for her because she made it look so easy.

"BE QUICK TO LISTEN AND SLOW TO SPEAK."

I don't remember her shedding a tear.

My mind started to expand. What other knowledge is out there in the world that I do not know about? Who has the information that I seek? I started to listen more so I could miss all the bumps in the road on my journey. I hit quite a few already at twenty-two. I noticed that people have a lot to say if you let them talk. My kids would tell you that I am one of those people. However, I am the one pouring into them. Once the time come for me to learn from them, I will let them have the floor to speak. Yes! I have learned so much from my children as well. The way they think about different topics and daily life situations amazes me. The key is to listen before you even think about giving your opinion. Listen then speak.

This key ingredient has allowed me to be more aware of who's talking and why should I listen? I am able to discern if the information they are speaking to me is for me or not. Being a teenager, I did not understand why grown-ups would say the same thing over and over and over again. I realized that it was out of love and not to make the same mistake they had done.

ACTION STEP:

I want you to think about the words that someone has spoken to you out of love, but you really weren't trying to HEAR what they had to say. Write your answer below.

I don't want you to get it misunderstood, I am not saying every word an older person speaks to you, your to do what they say. However, when you are listening you can HEAR the words that are for you which you can use in your LIFE when someone is trying to give you their best advice!

_____

_____

_____

_____

_____

_____

_____

_____

_____

_____

_____

_____

_____

LESSON NUMBER TWO

"BREATHE! IT WILL BE OKAY."

"BREATHE! IT WILL BE OKAY."

When I was little girl I could not wait to be twenty-five. Twenty- five seemed to be the magic number for grown-ups. Well maybe it was just me growing up too fast. Anyways, the conversation that I had with my mother was from experiencing so many ups and downs in life. One minute I am working, all my bills where paid and my children had everything they needed, next I'm laid off, on welfare, and borrowing money from my mom. Oh, and did I tell you that I was not a good picker of men.

Since I did grow up faster than most from having responsibilities as a teenage mother, by the time I was twenty -five I realized life was going to keep happening. What I mean is sometimes things were just out of my control. Then there were those things that were in my control.

I started reading self-help books that where life changing such as "Think and Grow Rich" by Napoleon Hill. " No Matter W hat", by Lisa Nicolas and "The Compound Effect" by Darren Hardy are just a few books that I read when realizing how I had a responsibility of the things that are in my control that I should handle.

I do have control over the food I put in my mouth. I do have control over the people I hang with. I do have control over the information I put in my mind to make me better at my job or business. I do have control over how much sleep I get. I do have control over how I spend my money. I do have control over how many men I sleep with. I do have control over how I give back to the world. These are just a few things that are in my control. I learned the HOW- TO steps for the things that are not in my control. The first thing is BREATHE! Learning how to breathe in situation that are not in your control helps you relax so that you can figure out the next step or solution to the situation.

Things are going to happen, but it is not the end of the world. You may fail a test. Ok. See if you can retake the test. If not, how can you be more prepared for the next one. Or perhaps you broke your phone. Ouch! It may be the end of your social media world for a day, week, or month, but it is not the end of the world. What else can you do in that time until the situation changes back in your favor. Just breathe! Understand things are going to happen in life, but don't lose your cool just because things did not go your way. Your phone broke? Imagine a tornado coming through and destroying your house. Oh, I forgot you do not have a house. Your parents do! They would be the ones that have to keep their cool the best way possible in the horrific situation, to better find a solution in the crisis. And, a tornado did destroy our house. Four years later I can say my family and I are okay! You to, will be okay with your new phone.

We may not like the outcome or feeling of getting laid off, losing someone we love, failing a test, being hurt in an accident, having to do someone else's chores, having to read, being told what to do, getting dumped by someone you really like, being teased or not having your mother in your life. After some horrifying situations, we got to keep moving and just know EVERYTHING WILL BE OKAY!

"BREATHE! IT WILL BE OKAY."

ACTION STEPS:

Write down your list of the things that are in your control now.

_____
_____
_____
_____
_____
_____
_____
_____
_____
_____
_____
_____
_____
_____
_____
_____
_____
_____
_____
_____

LESSON NUMBER THREE

"MISTAKES ARE BLESSINGS!"

Have you ever made a Mistake? When you made the mistake did you blurt out, "Wow what a blessing?" Well I haven't either. However, **"Mistakes are Blessings!"** At the time of the mistake it may not feel that way. Especially if it is a costly mistake.

A few months ago, I went out of town. I left my vehicle at home and my son decided to pick up a few of his friends and go to the store. As I was about five hours away coming back home, my father calls telling me that my son was stopped on side the road in my car. My dad had to push him home with his car. The key switch was broken. As I was driving back home all I could think about was what was going on through his mind.

I knew exactly what was going on. I could recall on my 15th birthday taken my mom's car while she was out of town to go over my cousin house to borrow some shoes. I had a friend in the car and on our way back home less than 2 miles away, I rear ended a four door sedan. I was very scared. Not scared that I hit the car in front of me. I was scared of what my mom was going to do to me.

Having time to breathe and think about the consequences of his action, I knew he thought he could go to the store and come back without me knowing. I knew he was scared. Knowing what he was feeling plus considering how he was a good kid that just made bad choice. I'd hope he had time to think about his actions before I returned home. I wanted him to know that he made a mistake. The mistake that he made does have consequences and should remain as a onetime mistake. If he learns from this mistake that it is not okay to take things that does not belong to you and does not do it again then the lesson is learned.

Thinking that you're going to get away with something does not make it right to do. As a matter of fact, it should be an indication that you should not do it.

The blessing in this particular mistake is that no one got hurt. Also, I was out of a car for about two months. He could see the domino effect of his actions.

I received a lesson from his actions as well. I learned that even though I could have been angry in the matter, I chose to be understanding instead of going off. If I was home when he had taken the car without having five hours to think, this story could be totally different. I learned that we all have room to grow. Most times that growth comes through experience. However, if his actions did not change that is where the problem would lay.

Your parents have certain standards for you based on their experiences. You may not understand it, but that's where communication comes in for you to talk with them to get an understanding. Then you still may not understand, that's when you should try to believe that they have your best interest in mind. Communication is key. Your mistakes matter when you look at the lesson within it.

ACTION STEPS:

What mistake have you made that you have learned a valuable lesson from? Do you see the blessing in the mistake? What would you do different? Write it down on below.

LESSON NUMBER FOUR

"GROWING NEVER STOPS?"

Have you noticed that you do not look the same from five years ago? What about ten years ago, do you still look the same? Do you know that **"GROWING NEVER STOPS?"** This is for everyone. Physically, emotionally, mentally, spiritually, financially are all part of the growing cycle in this generation. You should know more then you did when you were in elementary school until now right? Even after you finish your education, there is still growing to be done. Let's just talk from the stand point of you feeding your mind. Your mind is where all your decisions are made. It is your thinking tank. Those thought can evolve over time through life's experiences. One thing about experiences is that everyone has them. So, not only can you grow from your experiences, but you can also grow from other people experiences. You can look around you to collect information and you can read books to collect more information. Something that is more popular these days are videos. Looking at videos to grow so that you can expand your mind. There are so many ways we can continue to grow.

    I remember growing up I was able to see my step sister be the captain of the cheer team, get straight A's in school, go to college, graduate, get married and have a successful career. This was an example of a model, in a positive direction that I was able to witness. I once read a book that talked about a young woman being teased in school and how she did not feel beautiful. I connected with her because I was teased as well. I too did not feel beautiful. In the book she talked about

looking in the mirror, looking into her eyes and telling herself, "I Love You." I then thought this lady was crazy, but deepdown inside I wanted to love myself too. I started this process of saying "I love you" to myself every day in the mirror. The first couple of times I cried. Now about ten years later I love myself with a knowing sense that I say who I am, and whatever I say or believe about myself that is true for me, period.

The key in this lesson is to never stop growing. I hope you consider the fast tracks to growth, which are having a positive model, reading, research through video and then there are also seminars & conferences that you can attend to continue this process. Growing never stops!

"GROWING NEVER STOPS?"

ACTION STEPS

In what way beside school can you continue to grow yourself each day?

_____
_____
_____
_____
_____
_____
_____
_____
_____
_____
_____
_____
_____
_____
_____
_____
_____
_____
_____

LESSON NUMBER FIVE

"LIFTING YOURSELF UP VS. BEATING YOURSELF"

Did you know that you can hurt yourself with words? Did you know that you can feel amazing with your words? I would like to share the idea of **"Lifting yourself up vs. Beating yourself,"** so that you are aware of how your inner self talk does matter!

As I was growing up I heard the phrase that you are crazy if you talk to yourself. I bought into this idea. As an adult I realized how negative my thoughts were toward myself. My mouth was not opening, but in my mind, I was having a whole conversation. I was very rude. I was angry. I talked negative about other people. I talked bad about myself such as my nose was too big and my thighs where even bigger. I would beat myself up over the wrong choice I had made. This voice inside of my head was very loud. It created depression. Who wants depression? I did not. I had fallen so deep into depression listening to my own voice, you know the voice they say you're crazy if you talk to yourself. I would sleep most of my evenings away to shut the voice up. It wasn't until I got into business where my inner conversation started to change. This is where I learned about affirmations.

"LIFTING YOURSELF UP VS. BEATING YOURSELF"

Similar to the book I read that talked about looking in the mirror and telling yourself, "I Love You!" The business taught me personal development, which is how to develop myself as a person. Reading self-development books, going to conferences and seminars I heard a lot of the same thing. One of the things that I heard consistently was "Affirm your life!" Speak over your life, your business and family. We talk to ourselves all day long, but are we strategic about it

Let's try it now! Affirm these 5 saying aloud:

- **I am Beautiful**
- **I am powerful**
- **I am smart**
- **I am loved**
- **I am valuable**

Now who are you talking to? It is a wonderful feeling! It makes you feel great if you are actually putting feelings behind your words.

I thought about all the negative things that I had been saying to myself and I decided to change the way I talk. When I made a mistake, I would let myself know "It is okay, and things will get better." My goal would be to make sure I lift myself up that day if and when a mistake was made instead of beating myself up for days or even weeks.

What are you telling yourself about you? I would really want you to take the time to think about it. Are you saying things that lift you up on a daily basis? Or are you fighting yourself with your inner conversation like an enemy? It is okay if this has been your inner conversation we all have done it. However, it is not okay to continue this path. You can lift yourself up by the words you are speaking in your mind. If you know that there has been a negative thought process in your mind, don't focus on those thought but change them to a positive thought. Example:

Change - I am a bad person + To I am a great successful person in all my ways now!

Change - I am not good enough + To I am the best me that I can be now!

Change - I don't know how + To I am a great researcher of information now and I do not give up!

ACTION STEPS:

Write out your positive thoughts below and affirm them every day!

LESSON NUMBER SIX

"EVERY DECISION COUNT!"

Big or small **"EVERY DECISION COUNT!"** Yes! Even the things that we think are small are big! I was invited to have unlimited pancakes the other day. A few weeks ago, this idea would have sounded great. However, the results that I wanted was not in alignment with having the unlimited pancakes. When I told her that I was not able to attend with her because of my weight loss journey, her reply was "Oh girl I've been trying to lose weight for 40 years!" Instantly I thought, "Not one more day will I try, I will do!" I can see my end result if I did not stick to my decision. I would be telling someone the same thing forty years from now.

    I like to take every aspect of my life from my faith, family, fun, fitness, and finances to see what decision has been made that I can make better. When I study for a business project, I know that it will make me better in my finances eventually. From my experiences self-evaluating is the key for your next decision. Can I be honest with you? I used to make the same decision each day that were not healthy for my body nor my mind. It got so bad it effected my positive self-talk. However, my will power to win in life is so powerful, I was able to eventually lift myself out of the daily bad cycle. I decided that I can make great healthy choices. I made the decision not to go back into the cycles. I affirmed it daily. I knew that decision from

"EVERY DECISION COUNT!"

not having a bad diet or going back and forth in old relationships, could help with my overall lifestyle.

Many times, we do not think about how one decision can affect us and the people around us. Being observant before a decision is made, can help you make better choices in the future.

ACTION STEPS:

List 5 choices you have made in the past that has gotten you where you are today. Name 3 decisions that you have made to be better than you were yesterday.

_____
_____
_____
_____
_____
_____
_____
_____
_____
_____
_____
_____
_____
_____
_____
_____
_____
_____
_____

LESSON NUMBER 7

"EVERYONE HAS AN OPINION!"

Do you know when you look around a room everything that you see came from someone's mind? Look around the room right now. It all came from someone's thought. They did not need you to say it was okay to create it. They just created without your opinion. That is why it is important to know that **"EVERYONE HAS AN OPINION!"**

This is a valuable lesson because we are all unique individuals. We all have ideas floating in our brains about this book right now. Either you like it, or you don't. However you may feel, did not stop me from writing it and however you may feel may not stop the next persons opinion either. I want you to understand that once you have decided to choose a path to take in life, whether it be to attend college or not to attend college, if it be to get married or not get married, or if it is to work for a great company or start a business, it is a decision that you have chosen. Along your path there may be some people that will disagree with those decision.

Once I decide to be a believer in Christ, and follow his ways, there where some people that I was close with that did not understand, and our relationship change drastically. It went from hanging out every day to not even having their contact number. I was always a believer however, I did not strive to follow the way of GOD completely. I know that they are believers too, but I wanted my actions to speak louder than words. I realized that their new opinion of me could not stop me on my new journey. Although I wanted to hang out, we just did not click like we use to. My thoughts now are if someone such as myself is striving to be better and the people around me do not agree, then it is the end of my journey with them. Once I realized this heart hurtful lesson I was okay with letting people go.

Some will stick around to watch you fall on your face. YES, some family and friends will sit back and watch you fail miserably so they can go back and tell others. The truth is we are going to have some failures. You are going to make some mistakes. How you recover from them should be your only focus. You get up and try again.

So, with my experience of deciding on a path and then losing some family and friends that I use to hang around, I have learned to respect others opinion. We cannot see inside someone's head. IF I tell you to draw a picture of a dog in the next one minute, you're not going to draw the same dog that I imagined in my mind. From religion, careers, diets, fun, business, work ethic, all means something different to each of us. So in a persons mind, when we talk about fun, one person might see fun as relaxing on the beach for hours, while another person may be adventurous wanting to hike and swim with the dolphins. It is best to communicate your opinion and never be afraid to share because your opinion is different.

So yes, everyone has an opinion and we can learn, grow and change. However, growth happens on purpose. Everyone does not grow at the same pace. If you feel yourself growing faster than others, don't shrink back to fit in, keep going! You will find other like-minded people as you continue to level up your thinking. Others input do not matter when you have a vision in your mind that they cannot see. Be well with being the best version of yourself.

"EVERYONE HAS AN OPINION!"

ACTION STEP

What decisions have you made that others did not understand, but you saw it in your mind? Write it down below.

_____
_____
_____
_____
_____
_____
_____
_____
_____
_____
_____
_____
_____
_____
_____
_____
_____
_____

LESSON NUMBER EIGHT

"MONEY IS A TOOL"

You can learn the easy way or the hard way. "Money is a tool!" It is a necessity in our generation.

Do you remember when I was talking about how everyone has an opinion? Well I grew up in a family where the income was limited and we barley had enough at the end of the month. As a kid you could not tell me that we were in poverty. We always had food, shelter, clothes, we always had a great time with family and friends. We lived a great life I thought. But according to the stats, we were not living average, we were one of the low-income families. As I got older I realized what everything meant. I grew up in a single parent home and my mom had to do everything, from the rent, utilities, life insurance, car insurance, medical insurance, food, clothes, and whatever else you can name. Now I too had my children living in a low-income environment. I was the one who decided to fill out the leasing application and say here is where we will live. The other factor to that equation was it was the only place I knew of at the time that I could afford on my McDonalds earnings. As time went on I got a good paying job and decided to move my family to a better environment. That lasted until the job decided to let me go. It was at that point I realized the value of money and what it

"MONEY IS A TOOL"

can do for me, my family, and my community. It wasn't until I had no clue of how to earn it, that I could think of everything I NEEDED the money for.

I mention when I was younger I could not tell that we were in a low-income environment, because we never went without and my Mom made sure we always had a happy uplifting home. I say that to say that when people say money is not everything, it isn't, but it is and here is what I mean. If you know anyone that has been sick or couldn't leave the house due to their illness, money is not at the top of their list, that persons HEALTH is. The most important thing to that person is being well. In my opinion, HEALTH is everything. On the other hand, if we look at money as a tool, a TOOL that can give us everything that we need when in good health and better health care needs. It is a tool for our everyday life. Everything that you see in your home was bought with money. If it was a gift it was bought with someone else's money. We can do a lot with money when we use it for what it is needed for plus for our fun stuff as well.

ACTION STEPS:

I would like for you to write out a list of things that you would buy if you had $100,000 right now. Remember that money is a tool which you can use for the things you desire and need. Also think of the people or organizations that you will give to if you posses the money you desire now. Write them down.

LESSON NUMBER NINE

"GUIDE YOUR MIND"

If you want to guide your life "Guide Your Mind." Your mind is one of the greatest tools you own. It is how we go after the things we truly desire in life.

When my job let me go, I just knew I would get another job really fast. I thought I could get hired on with a company. Any company would have worked. I thought I'd just work my way up to a higher position. Two things happen: It took me about three months to find another job and I did not like the job. I was still young with growing boys that I had to take care of. All I could think about was making sure they had everything they needed. I did not have time to think about things like "What do I really want to do?" or "What is my life's purpose?" I can say at the time, age 22, my thoughts was to make sure my family had the things that they needed. That is where my mind took me. ***After learning that I have power to guide my mind to where I wanted to go, I had to figure out exactly where did I really want to go in life!*** At that time, I thought about moving into a supervisor role. There was an opening and I knew I could get the job done. I was on time every day. I did not miss any days, I knew I was in the door. Lo and behold they gave the job to someone else. Someone who I felt was not qualified because they took off so many days of work. Anyway, I talked with my manager and he told me to go after a position I had no experience in. I felt at the time, it wasn't the best decision for me to make. I would have been a supervisor over an area I never worked before. While I was talking with him he also was sharing with me that my hours were about to change. I had perfect working hours for a single mom which where 7a.m. to 4p.m. He told me I would have to work rotating shifts, or I could not work there anymore. Wow I thought!

We can look at life issues as a negative or a positive. Even though I did not like what I was feeling when my manager said what he said, I had to believe that their was something better for me. Now, I am so happy and grateful for his words because I would not be on my entrepreneur path that I am on today! Shortly after I left that job, I received a text message about a **life changing opportunity**. At that time I had no clue what an opportunity was. With that opportunity I had a chance to buy products at wholesale and sale it for retail. I started reading books on business where I learned that the mind will expand on whatever I focus on. What I focus on expands! I found my true purpose in life edifying and promoting women and young ladies with products and services.

My mind went passed working my way to the top of a company to having my own company. Everything that happened to me lead to where I am today. I believe that nothing just happens. I use my mind to take me **everywhere I want to go on purpose**. The mind is vital to your success in life. Whatever success is to you! I love sharing information with others to grow them and impact their lives. So, my mind doesn't take me to a job, it takes me to create another idea, or call another company, student, school, or church to speak to their audience. I did not use my mind as much as I do now. I was pregnant at 16, I wasn't thinking. Having my own business at 25, I started thinking about a lot of things. There are blessings in mistakes and

"GUIDE YOUR MIND"

I wouldn't change anything!

You cannot change what has happen to you, but you can use your mind today to go toward a direction on purpose for a great future. So now after this lesson you will be able to notice your thoughts. Whether your thoughts are positive or negative that is where you are going.

ACTION STEPS:

Write down the things you have been thinking about for your career. Write down how you can expand on those thoughts about your career.

LESSON NUMBER TEN

"IF YOU DO NOT KNOW SOMETHING YOU CAN FIND THE ANSWER"

Things are changing so fast in society to where sometimes it is hard to keep up with everything. In the mist we also have this great technology. Another lesson of mine is, **"IF YOU DO NOT KNOW SOMETHING YOU CAN FIND THE ANSWER."**

I notice that when one of my children come ask me a question about their school work, there was no research before coming to me. When they want to look up stats on a football player, they have no trouble searching different sites to find out the score, or the record of yards of a player. I quickly would let them know, "Just how you look up such and such player you can look up the answer to your homework. Then if you need help afterwards I'll be right here sweetie."

It would be nice if the answers could be given to us right away, but that takes away the learning aspect of life. How bad do you want it? When I was in the process of writing my first book I had no clue of anything. How to find an editor? What to look for when I am looking for an editor? Do I find a publisher or self-publish? All of the answers to my questions were found through a book, a mentor, or online video from YouTube. Next thing I know I was a self-published author on Amazon.

With determination and willingness to find the answers you seek to your success all depended upon you. Look at your vision, keep the vision in front of you, this will help you have the want-to-it-ness to master the art of finding answers for your dream. The answers are there. The great thing about learning is that you cannot unlearn it. ***Once you study it and implement, you know it!***

"IF YOU DO NOT KNOW SOMETHING YOU CAN FIND THE ANSWER"

ACTION STEPS:

Think about what you need answers to. Write down three ways you can research your answers. Then afterwards implement your research to get the answer.

_____
_____
_____
_____
_____
_____
_____
_____
_____
_____
_____
_____
_____
_____
_____
_____
_____

LESSON NUMBER ELEVEN

"PEACE IN YOUR MIND IS BETTER"

Life happens! People leave out of your life, we gain new friendships, we lose things, and new stuff comes in our life. It is my belief, **"PEACE IN YOUR MIND IS BETTER!"** You may be asking, "Better than what?" Peace in your mind is better than anything that you are attached too! Which sometimes means distancing yourself from family, friends, job, or school, or whatever that could be causing chaos for you.

Please understand what I am saying. If you have a class that is giving you mental toughness and the work is hard doesn't mean you drop the class. What you could do is see if there is tutoring available. You check to see if you could study with friends and actually study! It means not going out or not watching your favorite Tv show so that you could get your work turned in. Communication could solve a lot of cases, but when it doesn't help you may have to separate from distractions in order to keep peace.

I can remember one time when I had a disagreement with my sister. It was pretty ugly. My sister was my best friend. However, she was not seeing thing my way and I did not see things her way. At the place I was in my life, the situation caused me to be uneasy in my spirit. A few months went by and we were able to finally have a conversation. I can understand her perspective, but totally disagree. We don't talk like we use to, but there is communication which I am grateful for. It was the letting go to have peace that created what we have today. Otherwise we would be still at each other's throat.

I've been asked this question before, "Charlette, what if the person is my mother that I need to distance myself from?" I have shared with several women that we should always respect out parents. I believe in not arguing with my parents not even a lit a bit. I told one lady that you are an adult, one thing that we do have control over is what we do with our time. If you're an adult that's moved out the house, your parent should not still control your life. Key words, "adult" and "out the house." You can develop methods on dealing with your mom. We know that some people are going to always be who they are. This is actually an advantage. You know your parents. If you are in the household with them, you can go to your room. You can suggest counseling. Or if you're out of the house you may try not to visit for a while until you are able to handle the words and action of your mother. We all want real answers in sensitive situations. Truth is there will be trouble in our life. There is no need to run when instead we can figure the situation out. There is help with resolving the issue by you taking responsibility of the situation, putting your feelings and emotions in check, so that you can implement a strategy to see what the right solution for you is.

I also want to note that I am not a license professional to be able to give you professional advice. Everyone situation is different. If you are having issues you should seek professional help. The information is based on experiences of the writer.

ACTION STEPS:

Is there a relationship that needs to be restored in your life? Did you over react in the situation? Write how you could have handled the situation better? In what way can you implement a strategy to make the relationship better.

LESSON NUMBER TWELVE

"LOVE OTHERS AS YOURSELF"

Have you ever heard the saying treat others as the way you want to be treated? I heard this a lot growing up. What I never thought about though was how do I want to be treated. Looking back, I wished I thought more about how to love myself more and to treat people exactly how I would like to be treated. **"LOVE OTHERS AS YOURSELF."**

    The first thing that I learned about love is that even when I did not love myself, someone loved me! How did I know that they love me? I knew that they loved me because how they treated me as an individual. They made sure I was taking care of to the best of their ability. This person was my mom. I knew my mom loved us. One thing that I wished I had more of was hugs. So, the thing I implemented with my three sons was that we hug when we see each other and when we depart. This add- on of hugs is a way I thought could enhance how to show love and to feel loved. I showed them this is how I would like to be treated.

    A friend of mine and I would often have lunch together a few times when our schedules would match up. When we meet she always had a gift for me. She has given me bracelets, books, journals, oils and prayers. Each time though I felt surprised. I also felt valued and loved. Not just because she purchased or made me something, but because she intentional thought of who I was for the item she picked out. She knew I would enjoy the bracelets and books that she picked out for me. It was a kind act that she made which made me feel loved.

I remember one time walking into work one day and as I came around the corner my coworkers greeted me with a jaw dropping expression on her face of WOW you look gorgeous! Before the words even came out of her mouth I could see it on her face. It was real and genuine. She really meant what she said. I felt the love from her thoughts of me. It was all over her face.

Love means different things for everyone. I found the kind of love that I wanted to show to myself and to others. Love that would be real, genuine, with hugs and unexpected gifts. Love is an action. When I look in the mirror, I do not look to see what wrong is with me. I affirm myself with love affirmations in the mirror in the morning time. Similar to how my coworker reacted to me, I react the same way when I speak to myself in the mirror. It is a feeling of joy. Especially for the days when I do not feel loved. I remind myself that I am loved! I am Beautiful! I am the bomb dot com. Not to brag when I am out in public, but to myself humbly exclaiming to myself in private that, "I am a great creation*!" **Since I know how to create love within, I can show it without to others!**

"LOVE OTHERS AS YOURSELF"

ACTION STEPS:

Write down the seven ways you show love to yourself. Think about how you have been treated by another person that really made you feel loved. Write down what they did? How did it make you feel on the inside? Also, how can you add more self-love in your daily routine?

LESSON NUMBER THIRTEEN

"EXCELLENCE IS A HABIT!"

Aristotle thought "We are what we repeatedly do. Excellence, then is not an act but a habit?" What I took from his quote is **"EXCELLENCE IS A HABIT!"**

If you could remember learning your ABC, it was a process that may have started before grade school. It was a daily morning, afternoon, and evening homework routine. It is the foundation of the English language. Repetition was the key to remember the letters of the alphabets. Now, you do not have to pause and think of the next letter when speaking or singing your ABC's. You may haven't even said your alphabets in a long time, but you still remember them.

Repetition creates habit! If I wanted to be excellent in my endeavors, I had to create the repetition of whatever it was that I wanted to be excellent in. One of the first thing I wanted to be excellent in was being a great mother. I would often think how my kids did not ask to be here and it was my responsibility to create a safe loving environment for them. I witness other mothers, unfortunately that did not take the responsibility of taking care of the child's basic needs. I wanted more so I created more.

We all have the ability to look at our life and say I want to be

"EXCELLENCE IS A HABIT!"

greater in this area, then put in the necessary work to be excellent. With much practice I have become a better communicator. I make it an effort to be better each day. I used to stutter which cause me to have low self- esteem. Every time I would talk to someone they would look at me with a blank look on their face. They would ask me to repeat what I said. It happened so often that I just would say never mind to what I said. My business model now includes me doing presentations, workshops, and transformational speaking! I speak to clients, students mostly everyday in some form without thinking of stuttering. Now, if I slip up I keep going. In the past it happened so often because I was focused on if I was going to stutter. Remember whatever you focus on expands.

Giving up is not an option for whatever you truly desire. Practice your craft each day so that you can be better. Even the greatest athletes still practice! Stephen Curry, Lebron James, Serena Williams know the importance of going to practice because it is geared toward their excellence performance each time they are on the court. These players make millions of dollars and still value PRACTICE. When I googled the word practice it means: the customary, habitual, or expected procedure or way of doing of something. It is a habitual way of doing something.

ACTION STEPS:

Think of an area that you would like to be excellent in. Write out ways that you can create a habit for that area and then put it into practice each day!

LESSON NUMBER FOURTEEN

"CONSISTENCE IS KEY"

As you build on being excellence it is easy to roll back into our old habits. It is important to stay consistent. *You have been doing your regular routine all your life and now when you decide you want to be better, you have to purposely make it a happen.* Do it until it is something that you do automatically just like your ABC. **"CONSISTENCE IS KEY!"**

Someone once told me, you are consistently inconsistent. I thought it was a profound comment that after hearing it elevated me to be better. He was absolutely right. At the time consistence was an area that I was trying to improve. I would work out for a few months and then stop for about three months then start right back. This went on for a while. Not only within my workout routines, but also in my study habits and my personal relationships. To have someone to look in from the outside to share the words to help me realize I was consistent, at being inconsistent, I just needed to make a shift. The shift in my mind was to just keep performing in all areas of life no matter what happens so that I could be established in my goals.

The experience taught me to be clear in my decisions. *If a decision is made I should stand in that decision even through life negatives or positive situations, or even if my feelings change.* If you say that you want to complete your degree, but during mid finals you find myself overwhelmed don't quit, take a moment to breathe and remember why you want this. Then complete it! Clarity is everything especially in the mist of emotions and pain.

    The consistency comes from being clear on your desired outcome. It is easier to stay on a path when you are clear about what you want. I always refer back to Michael Jordan's flu game. He was sick with body ache, fever, chills, and played one of the best games of his life! He knew exactly what he wanted! I like to think about how he overcame in the moment of his pain! It is astonishing to me that he pushed through, because sometimes when I have a headache I want to stop working and lay down to sleep. However, after SEEING what some might think to be impossible in Michaels Jordan game, I can now muster up the strength to keep going no matter how weak I may feel. I keep the goal in front of me. You get it! GOAL… In Front.

"CONSISTENCE IS KEY"

ACTION STEPS:

Write down your goals for the year below. Keep them in front of you. This will help you be clear to stay on the path. Remember "Consistency is the key!"

LESSON NUMBER FIFTEEN

"BE"

Who are you? I remember when this question was asked to me. I thought I was me! I am me. Why would anyone that know me ask me that question? It is a big deal! Who are you? My son would say that I am MOM. My sister would say I am Sister. We all have these roles that we play in people's life. I realized when my mom passed I am no longer her daughter. Things changed instantly for that role in my life. I thought about the "Who are you?" question that was asked to me years before. Who am I today? I am Charlette!! I am being the best version of myself in all areas! The key in this lesson is not to get caught up in titles because titles can change just like when my mother died! Just

"BE!"

I spoke to my oldest son Cameron's tenth grade class. I ask them the question

"Who Am I?" Some said Charlette and others said Cameron's Mom! This is why it is important for you to BE who you are, because everyone has an idea of who you are. I was Charlette before I became Cameron's mom. I am Cameron's mom, but I am Charlette first. I wasn't in the role at the school of being Cameron's mom. I came to speak and empower the youth

"BE"

at that moment. I was BEING me. When I get home and tell Cameron to clean his room or take the trash out I am in the role of being his mom which is a part of who Charlette is.

At the beginning of my marriage I went through an identity crisis. I had Been Charlette White for my whole life. Being married was bigger than a role being change. My identity was changed. I had to adapt a whole new name.

I knew I wasn't the first woman to feel this way. I found out there where a lot of women who at the beginning of their marriage asked the question, who am I? Once they answered they said Who is that? Sounds funny, but it was real.

At this moment take in a deep breath, then exhale. This is the present moment! This is who you are. The past is gone, and the future hasn't happened yet. ***There are stages to you.*** I know if you are reading this that you are not a baby. You may be a student, learning to improve yourself, so that you can have a great career. After that you will evolve into a different version of yourself after you obtain your degree.

However, in this moment if you choose right now that you can BE better, you can continue to sit and take deep breathes to imagine what does that person look like! What would you be doing? How do you feel? Practice Being it!

ACTION STEP:

What do you think about the most: your past, your present, or the future? Over the next several days think about how you can just BE more focused in the moment. As you do this you will feel more freer and not limited to time. Do this then leave a review on my social media of how this worked out for you. #CharletteTheChallenger

LESSON NUMBER SIXTEEN

"IMAGINE YOUR GREATNESS"

As you can see, the lessons are tied together. In this lesson I would like for you to **"IMAGINE YOUR GREATNESS!"** A mentor told me that you do not get what you want out of life, you get what you picture! He asked "What picture do you have in your mind." His company hosted different events. At this particular event he said that he already seen his next three events that was in the next year. Immediately my mind expanded!

Imagination allows our mind to expand. It also allows us to see the possibilities so that we can act on them now. Before I was speaking at schools I already seen it in my mind. I was clear of what I wanted. I couldn't see it in my reality, however it was in my mind before it ever happened. As I mentioned earlier that YOU go where ever your mind takes you. Our thoughts are so powerful that we can create in our mind then bring the idea out of the mind into the world we live in and see! As you are in class, or on your job, or even when you are at home you are creating your future through your imagination.

I teach a course called 21 days of speaking over your life. For the past 2 years it has been a great success! It is a free course! You may say how is it a success? Success does not always equal money. It was a success from the feedback I received from the participants that showed up every day! The mission was for people to implement the information that I was giving to them. Once they speak over their life there would be a positive shift at the end of the 21 days they could see. This is what I saw in my mind. That someone would have an experience of seeing what they spoke come into existing. The second year two people shared how what they said came to pass. They felt uplifted and will continue to go through the process of speaking over their life. It works! By them sharing their story with me gave me a boost of confidence to continue, because I saw what I imagine come to reality! When I received confidence, it makes the conviction much stronger when I do other projects. I now have more belief to imagine the next project and watch it come true.

"IMAGINE YOUR GREATNESS"

ACTION STEPS:

What are you imagining for your success? Do you doubt that it could happen? Write down your doubts. Then with a pen I would like for you to draw a line through each doubt and remember it no more. It is important to cancel out all the doubt. *Faith and fear can't be in the mind at the same time. One has to dominate the other. Both requires you to use your imagination. Only imagine your end result.* Write down your end result.

_____

_____

_____

_____

_____

_____

_____

_____

_____

_____

_____

_____

_____

_____

LESSON NUMBER SEVENTEEN

"BE BOLD AND COURAGEOUS!"

To have Victory takes Boldness and Courage! This key lesson is for you to activate your bold faith and act courageous in that process! A scripture that I often read is **"BE BOLD AND COURAGEOUS!"** I can share that the boldness that I had as a teen, I still have it to day. It is just on a different level. Instead of being in the streets, I am using my boldness in business.

Yes, you read correctly, in the streets. Do you want the truth or a lie? The term streets on the street is when a person may be doing illegal activates to earn their income. It took courage for me to say no, and live another way. I wanted to be different! I would think, " I must do something different!" Even though it was for a short while, it is easy to get in trouble. One afternoon I went outside to check on two of my boys and as I shut the door behind me, out the corner of my eye, I saw a police officer at my door with his gun drawn. I looked down the steps on one side there where serveral polices on the ground with their guns out. I look the other way I could see three police cars. At that moment all I could think about were my two little boys. The police asked me about the gentleman that just entered in my house. I let the officer know that yes a man was inside that fits the

"BE BOLD AND COURAGEOUS!"

description and that there are two men in the apartment in one was my boyfriend. The officer said move out the way. So, I ran down the step to get my boys. This was the scariest moments of my life. My family was in harm's way due to my poor decision. There was no one to blame I knew better. I had to act to separate myself from the situation.

I am not perfect, but my mistakes definitely helped me be bolder to step into the positive adventures in my life. I believed that GOD told me to promote others on a platformed called Victory TV in 2018. Not knowing how, I started the process! I've done many interviews with authors, community leaders, business leaders and others that are impacting the community. These leaders have no clue of my pass! My pass does not determine who I am today! Did doubt try to creep in? Yes It did, but I canceled the thought, by saying "This thought has no place in my mind and I choose to believe in myself !" This is why the courage is so important. When you google the word courage it means the ability to do something that frightens one. There are going to be scary times but build on each opportunity to show your boldness and courage! Just like a muscle, each time you work it out, that muscle gets stronger and stronger.

ACTION STEPS:

How can you use your boldness muscle to get stronger? How can you have more courage in your activities?

LESSON NUMBER EIGHTEEN

"GIVING IS ONE OF THE GREATEST REWARDS"

If you happy and you know it clap your hands! This was a song as a little kid I loved to sing. I was always happy and when I clap my hands the energy was amazing! I learned that there is another way to create this happiness in my life and that is through giving! **"GIVING IS ONE OF THE GREATEST REWARDS!"**

As I'm doing spring cleaning, I threw away some old jeans. The jeans wasn't worth giving to the second hand store so I threw them in the trash. Hours later I remembered there was one buck in one of the pockets. I don't believe in throwing money away, so I had to dig through the trash, which was something I was not happy about, then lo and behold was the one-dollar bill. I said to myself this money is worth way more than it really is. A few days later I went to the gas station, there was a man outside who asked for money. Before I give to someone on the streets I like to think to myself first, "Is the person asking for the money really sincere or not." Well this gentleman looked serious as if he needed the money for what he said it was for. I gave him the dollar and the man start worshiping GOD. The man exclaimed the dollar was the exact amount he was short. His gratefulness made me feel this incredible feeling on the inside. The energy was bigger than the clapping of the hands. There was joy within me which lasted for days from giving this person one dollar!

Have you ever been surprised from a gift that you received? I had someone ask to borrow twenty dollars once. I knew if they were asking for twenty dollars that they really must needed it so instead I gave them one hundred dollars. The expression of gratitude was phenomenal. In this situation I knew exactly how they were feeling because I was in the same situation before when I had to borrow twenty dollars but received one hundred! **"GIVING IS ONE OF THE GREATEST REWARDS!"** The feeling is indescribable. One time I was at a fast food restaurant when a lady with her young daughters came inside, it was early and looked like the kids were dressed for school. The lady wasn't smiling so I looked at her with a huge smile on my face until she looked back at me. She gave me a half smile. I could tell she was having a ruff morning. However, I knew a smile could change a person mood once they put it on their face. Giving doesn't has to be money. It can be just a simple smile to make someone day.

"GIVING IS ONE OF THE GREATEST REWARDS"

ACTION STEPS:

Make a list of ways that you could give more. Your giving does not have to be things or money. It may be time as well. Write your list below.

_____

_____

_____

_____

_____

_____

_____

_____

_____

_____

_____

_____

_____

_____

_____

LESSON NUMBER NINETEEN

"YOU HAVE TO WANNA CHANGE"

When things do not seem like they are happening for you. This is not the time to get frustrated, just breathe again! It is a time for growth within yourself. We should always be progressing toward becoming better. In order for the progress to happen **"YOU HAVE TO WANNA CHANGE!"** No one can do it for you. You are the key to your own future!

Imagine if you were to stay the exact same way you are today. If nothing else changes about you such as your grade, your friends, your age, your size, your look, and your lifestyle, what would life be like? It wouldn't be very exciting because you'll know exactly what will happen each day! *You can tell your future by what you do today!*

When I was writing my first book, I sat down in my office each day until it was complete. I did not miss a day. Before I made the decision to write every day, I would write here and there whenever I could fit it in. *It wasn't until I made this book my top priority that I saw real results.* The result I wanted was for it to be complete.

I tell you to breathe again, cause if the results aren't showing up for you the way you would like, a mindset shift can be made in your plan. We

"YOU HAVE TO WANNA CHANGE"

are so eager to see progress we forget to be in the present moment where all the change is taking place. Right now! ***What is your next move after you put this book down? How will it make you feel when you do it? Is it getting you closer to your goal? Think on these things so that you won't repeat the same cycles.***

ACTION STEP:

Write down your main priority in your life right now. What movement needs to take place to get you closer to that goal?

LESSON NUMBER TWENTY

"BELIEVING IN YOURSELF"

A key ingredient to victory is "Believing in yourself!" I think we have this feeling on the inside one time or another when we wondered if we really could be great. I've heard one celebrity say he always believed in himself and that he believed in GOD the most. I do not know why my life story had a lot of doubt at the beginning, but I am thankful enough now to understand that the more I believe in myself the more I can bring transformation to not only my life but other people in the world.

I got over the fear of what others thought about me when I realized no matter if I am doing good things, I am still talked about. That is present tense. Some people only like to focus on the mistakes you made long time ago vs your current strides you are making. I got over the fear of speaking in front of an audience. Plus, I stopped being concerned with what others may think of me. I became so convinced about what I wanted!

It takes one opportunity for you to build confidence in yourself. If it is on an assignment that you weren't so sure about, but then you pass with a high grade it just boosted your confidence to another level. At the end of my eleventh-grade year I was determined to finish the year out even though I had my son two weeks before school ended. I was able to get my test so that I could make up my work. My goal was not to be a drop out because of the choice that I made. I brought a child into the world without being prepared to take care of a child mentally or financially. I remember one night I was really sleepy, so I asked my mom if she could watch my son. I was so happy she said yes. It was my first time in weeks sleeping through the whole night. As I look at my son he is a great blessing. I had to woman up and become a responsible being for him no matter what. I believe that I have raised him and his brothers to the best of my ability and can now share powerfully with other young adults, letting them know to wait to be prepared mentally and financially before bringing a child into the world.

Making all the thousands of mistakes I realized those mistakes grew me! I'm not perfect, but I am unstoppable! If you are willing to learn through mistakes you can grow so much faster to believe in yourself more. If you do not believe in yourself who will. Be willing to believe in yourself to victory!

"BELIEVING IN YOURSELF"

ACTION STEPS:

Are you willing to believe in yourself? Write down the area you want more belief and then create a belief affirmation below and speak it daily.

LESSON NUMBER TWENTY-ONE

"SUCCESS IS NOT GIVEN IT IS EARNED!"

Imagine you are outside and huge spider came toward you, what would you do? I would step on it so hard then twist my foot to make sure that it would not ever be able to come toward me again! Now imagine if you could step on your fear to make sure it could never come toward you again! I used to tell people that I moved forward scared! One thing I knew was I was going forward and not backwards! If I wanted any type of success I was going to have to earn it! **"SUCCESS IS NOT GIVEN IT IS EARNED!"**

We talked about fear earlier and we know it is not fun to have! Fear gets in the way of what we really want to do! Fear keeps us up at night. Fear threatens us not to walk down the long hallway. Fear stops us from trying! Imagine you stepping on that fear and using all your power to move through the fear! If you really want to be a success, you have to step on the things that are in your way. You have to block out the haters, your negative thoughts, the negative people, all of your flaws and go after what you know.

I asked myself, how hard are you willing to work for what you say

"SUCCESS IS NOT GIVEN IT IS EARNED!"

you want? I got to the point that I was willing to do whatever it takes to become the person I need to be to accomplish my goals. I stop playing and told myself to create the person who can get it done. I heard an Instagram Influencer share with his followers: " If you cannot do it yourself create the person who can!" In other words, create within yourself the person who can get the job done.

Everyone has a story. Everyone has flaws. Everyone is not perfect. You can get up and earn your place in your life. Meaning if your struggling in your class work you can get tutoring! But if you are worried what others are thinking because you need extra help, this means you still care what others are thinking about and are not willing to grow into your best self. You have to take what you want! This is a positive take! If you have access to a teacher that could help you with your work, take the opportunity. Thats a win! It is either win or lose!

ACTION STEPS:

Write down how you are willing to take your success? How can you create a better you right now? Write your answers below.

_____

_____

_____

_____

_____

_____

_____

_____

_____

_____

_____

_____

_____

_____

_____

_____

_____

LESSON NUMBER TWENTY-TWO

"QUIET TIME IS THE BEST TIME!"

Have you ever thought spending time alone as a way of caring for yourself? I found out that a lot of my answers did not come when I was around people, but when I was alone. **"QUIET TIME IS THE BEST TIME!"** Spending time with yourself allows you to know more about you. Have you ever heard someone say that they hate being alone? That person probably doesn't enjoy being with themselves. If you're that person that does not like being alone, you need to find out what you really enjoy about you! Get to know you. Since you are reading this book, reading can count as one of the things you like to enjoy. Reading is one of the ways I like to spend time with myself.

I was very annoyed the other day. I know bad days happen when I feel down, but I really wanted to snap out of it quickly. However, the techniques I was trying was not working. I had been working and studying for an upcoming project and writing this book for you. I am the type of person that likes to get things done. At this particular moment my body was saying NO you need to rest. This is what I needed, but did not want to face the fact. My mind needed a rest. I was unaware of it at the time. Also, as of today, as I am writing this particular lesson, the city of Dallas, TX has restrictions because of the coronavirus. Restaurants, schools, businesses, movie theaters are not operating at full capacity. I did not realize that the combination of things that was going on in the world plus my projects I was working on was taking a mental toll. So, I took a break for a few days from writing and then came back to this lesson. I thought it was ironic being on this lesson while having to get away from everything to regroup my mind. I received so many revelations about my next steps while being silent from the noise of the world. I was clear on what was happening next for me. Even though things were happening in the world were outside of my control, I stop feeding into all the news plus social media to narrow my focus on my main project. Since then I have been rejuvenated! Now I am updating myself about what's going on in the world. My job is to focus on the things that bring peace, that brings healing, that brings in more finances. Does the issue affects us? Yes! However, I choose not to let the circumstance make us. Us being my family. There is no fear here!

I have walked for the last 2 days outside my apartment complex! This is another way that I spend alone time with myself. Remember what you focus on expand. If we focus on the problem that problem will expand! If we focus on the on things that are pure, honest, and loving, our goals, our freedom that will be expanded. It is a choice though. I am choosing to make the necessary choices that are needed for my mind to grow in a season when it seems as if everything is dying on the outside. It is the inside that allows for beautiful things to happen on the outside. We create in our alone time. GOD has a way of bringing us closer to ourselves so that Victory can take place.

"QUIET TIME IS THE BEST TIME!"

ACTION STEPS:

Do you enjoy alone time? If the answer is no, write how you can start enjoying more alone time with yourself so that you can execute your goals. If your answer is yes, write out how you can find something new to do in your alone time.

LESSON NUMBER TWENTY-THREE

"GIVING THANKS IN EVERY SITUATION"

Someone asked me how do you do it? How do you continue to move forward despite the things that has happen to you? In the past 3 years I had my mom and my grandmother to pass. Most recently I was involved in a horrific car accident. I had practiced **"GIVING THANKS IN EVERY SITUATION"** prior to these life changing situations. When things are going well and when things do not go well I give thanks,because I know that it is working for my good. No one wants to lose a loved one, but it is going to happen. No one wants to be in a car accident, but accidents happen. I now understand that my mother and grandmother transition is a part of life. I understand that I still had life after the car wreck. Even though it hurts still give thanks!

When I think about giving thanks I imagine the American holiday, Thanksgiving. It is a time family come together and share their time and love with one another. It is a time to give thanks for the people that are in our life. The time that is shared creates so many memories that money cannot buy.

"GIVING THANKS IN EVERY SITUATION"

I like to think about things money cannot buy such as the air that we breathe, good family and friends, health, time, the plants and trees. When I wake up in the morning I am able to express thanks because I can SEE a brand-new day with breath in my body plus health and strength. We sometimes don't recognize those things until it is to late.

I know a lot of people that do not express thanks in every situation. They only do it when everything is going well for them. I would like for you to try and give thanks the next time something unpleasant happens to you. You may not immediately give thanks, but don't let 24 hours pass without you being thankful for the situation. In your thankfulness, your process of healing starts. The pain will start to reside, and you will be able to look at your situation that you thought was bad as working for your good. Now listen. I never said you would LIKE what has happened. The key is to give thanks so that the healing can take place and to have peace in your mind. Your way of being will be affected by what has happen based on how you control your emotions. Decided how you will see your circumstance. In my heart I know my mom would want me to not cry for her. I can't change what happened to her, so I just imagine that she is rooting for me to continue to move forward in life with a big smile on her face. I hope you choose to give thanks in your situation.

ACTION STEPS:

Write down your pain you remember. It can be anything. How can you be thankful in that situation? Then give thanks to it. Look from a perspective of how you are more aware or have better character from the pain.

_____

_____

_____

_____

_____

_____

_____

_____

_____

_____

_____

_____

_____

_____

_____

_____

_____

_____

LESSON NUMBER TWENTY-FOUR

"IT'S OKAY TO SAY NO"

"IT'S OKAY TO SAY NO!" Period! Plain and simple. WE are all humans. When you feel that something is not okay, or something is happening that is against your will it is okay to say NO! Whether it be friends or family your not obligated to do the thing that you do not agree with. Now listen! Understand that everyone does not have a home that is a safe environment. You however, should always respect the people that are raising you! You as a teen will not agree with doing your chores or your choice of punishment, but you must follow the rules. There is a difference in rules than feeling obligated to do something for someone when you really want to say no, but you say yes anyway.

    I used to be the yes person. I thought if I had said no, I would have been hurting the other persons feelings. In my heart I want that person to have whatever it was they wanted if I was able to give it to them. Meaning, in my mind I really did not want to do it and did it anyway. I would feel guilty if I did not do what was asked of me. I would feel bad if I told them no. I was so torn of what to do.

    Finally, I got to a point where I let my no be no and meant it. Without the guilt! My mind was able to handle the decision that I made no matter their expression. It was a freeing experience. I've even had people to get mad at me because I said no. I could not fulfill what they were asking of me. The lesson was that the person just assumed I was supposed to do what they asked of me. When I told them no they could not understand nor handle my choice.

We are not obligated to do things if we do not want to. Unless it is our parents or guardians. I have driven across town to make sure my mom had whatever she needed, if she asked. I actually wanted to do it. She raised me, took good care of me. Whatever she asked I most likely done without second guessing. People do not have to be nice. We choose to be nice. Some people do not respect that. You can place boundaries with people that do not respect your "NO." You should start respecting your "NO" as well.

"IT'S OKAY TO SAY NO"

ACTION STEPS:

If you're a yes person, how do you feel saying no to a person who ask something of you? Why would you feel that way? Write it below. Take note: Your "NO" should be respected just as they want you to respect what they are asking. Once you start speaking your truth, you will know who is really for you.

LESSON NUMBER TWENTY-FIVE

"BIRDS OF A FEATHER FLOCK TOGETHER"

It is true, **"BIRDS OF A FEATHER FLOCK TOGETHER!"** Let's really think about it. Eagles are with Eagles, Pigeons hangout with Pigeons, and Hippos hang with Hippos! The saying shows how if I like to fly high, I will hang out with the birds that like to fly high. If I am a bird that like to be stay on the ground I would hang out with the birds that are on the ground. And If I am an animal that like to bathe in the mud, I would hang out with other animals that do the same thing. Who do you hang out with? Do your friends like to study or get high? Are you and your friends the opposite of each other? What do you have in common with them? Think about the things you do together that make you guys alike.

    A young lady said, "When I was with my ex we smoked all day every day. I got into another relationship and we smoked sometimes when we were together. Then, when I got with my husband I never smoked. I found out that smoking was not really for me and I did it because I was hanging out with the guy I was with." As I look at her face I could tell she learned a lot from her experience. People can have an impact on us without us even

"BIRDS OF A FEATHER FLOCK TOGETHER"

noticing. She told me she is now very selective in choosing partnerships.

Many times, we stay around people because we grew up with those people our whole lives. People can outgrow each other. Everyone grows at a different pace. Imagine meeting a person in grade school that study every day, turn in their work on time, an honor student, know what they want to do with their life and actually do that, but you on the other hand done the opposite. You skipped class, you done just enough work to pass, and you do not know what you want to do with your life. The two people may still have love for each other, however they are definitely going in different directions.

When I met my father's family side at ten years old, a big shift happened in my life. I was able to see people live differently than the way I was used to. Family gathering to cooking to how they played together was totally out of my norm. I was able to see quickly at a young age that families have different lifestyles and depending on what you gravitate to, you will adapt that way of living. What you see from me today is something I took from both sides. My mom was very giving and a little shy. My dad was very giving and outgoing. I am very giving and outgoing. I used to be shy, but I grew out of it by PRACTING being outgoing. I watch my dad be able to talk to anyone everywhere we went. My mom side loves to bargain shop and my dad side likes name brand. Now as an adult, I love to bargain shop for my clothes and shoes, so I took after my mom's side of the family. Think about why you are the way you are?

We get to define what we want out of life. Look at your surroundings. Things can change at any moment. The big question is what will your change be? How will you act? Are you acting like everyone else? Flock with the people that are moving toward their goals in life. Flock with people that are emotionally strong. Flock with the people that can handle tough situation. Focus on being your best version of yourself and the people that will come into your life will be there for you indefinitely. Your circle matters.

ACTION STEP:

Write below if you are being your best self when around others. Also, write down if your character change hanging around certain people. If so how?

LESSON NUMBER TWENTY-SIX

"VICTORY IS ALREADY YOURS"

As you move through life there will be obstacles, distractions, confusion, things that you have no control over, but one thing is for **SURE "VICTORY IS ALREADY YOURS!"** Although you may not feel like it in the moment, you will get past the obstacle, the distractions, the confusion and the things you have no control over as long as you focus on solutions rather than complaining.

The whole reason this book was written was share with you that **"VICTORY IS ALREADY YOURS!"** The situation you may be facing you already have the Victory. There is a process to get to it. Many times, when I was younger I thought I would not make it through the hard times. I felt as if it was ridiculous, it was tough, and just could not see my way out! At the age of 22 I decided that I was not going to feel as if I could not make it through anymore. I made up in my mind that whatever seems tough in life that I was going to come out of it. Unwanted situations may come up, but the decision to go through the pressure of life required the mental endurance which I developed!

To even have victory a person must beat the odds. I've seen situations where two people went through the same thing, but both had different experiences. One had a rough experience and the other one had a great experience. My eleventh-grade computer teacher was very rude I thought. I used to dread going to her class. I do not know why, but she was the only teacher that I had an issue with in life. I am a believer that we go to class to learn, but for some reason I felt as if she was picking on me. After a while I became a little disturbed and I did not due work in her class for a while. She had told me that the information that she was teaching me would be very valuable to me. I now know what she meant, especially since I am typing the draft of my book in a word doc. The following year I had her class again. I experienced the same thing in her class. Looking back, I would love to meet with her today to let her know that she was right. Most of my businesses is online and I use word documents all the time. I now believe I should have continued learning without being disruptive in her classroom. I just did not understand it at that moment. This Victory lesson for me was understanding this teacher job was for me to learn the information and keep it moving.

There are many occasions now when I listen when someone older is speaking. I have heard while in conversation things that were pertaining to my life that I implemented right away. I have gotten out of relationships because a lady and I shared similar stories and I refused to go through what I was going through for many more years as she did. Her story made me believe in the possibility of not having to settle.

Victory comes in all shapes in sizes. Think of a championship game. Both teams made it to the championship game, but only one can be a winner. Think about how you can take the losses of your pass to win the championship of your now and future!

ACTION STEP:

What past experience do you consider a loss? Do you know what you would have done now if you had to do it all over again? Write down your advice that you would give to another young woman or man if the opportunity came for you to do so.

LESSON NUMBER TWENTY-SEVEN

"DON'T SETTLE"

During a game of monopoly, my son let another player have a dollar. I exclaimed, you just going to give him free money. His response was, "It's Just a dollar." Yes, it was a dollar however, in the real-life game of life we do not just give money away to help our competitors. We have to understand the value of what we have and why we have it before giving it away. Understanding your value is the key for you not to settle for anything. **"DON'T SETTLE,"** in this life! In order not to settle you have to know your worth.

Life is all about learning yourself and making the necessary changes if needed. As I reflect on my life I learn why I do what I do. Before we got a new fifth grade teacher, we would get rewarded for wearing our uniforms and for earning good grades in class. I was one of the top students in that class. Our teacher left in the middle of the year and I was not as ambitious as before because things had change. The new teacher was totally different. HE didn't give us any rewards for being on the honor roll. Nor did he give us rewards for wearing our uniforms. This was during the time when the school district was trying to implement the uniform program and we could wear uniforms if we wanted but we did not have too. My motivation was

"DON'T SETTLE"

gone. I did not have the same drive as before when I KNEW I was going to get a reward. Today, as I look back on this, I learned how I operate. I do things to be excellent. My reward now is completing the goal. I do not settle anymore based on what someone expects of me, but I show my worth of who I am in all the work I do.

Settling comes in many forms. You may not understand now, but your worth more than a sweet talk. You may ask what is sweet talk? You know the kind when a guy walks up to you, then tell you sweet things about yourself. Suppose he tell you how beautiful you are. Well if you have been doing your affirmations his wo rds shouldn't sweep yo u off your feet. Most time people settle in relationship because they do not know their worth. They wait for someone else to tell them. When you do not know your worth, you try to please others and just go with the flow of things. I remember this guy told me that I was simple. Simple as if he mentioned a restaurant to go to for dinner, I would say okay. If asked to go to the movies to watch such and such I would say yes. I wasn't objective. I was just yes to whatever! Long after that relationship ended, I found out who I was, what I liked and why I liked it. I do not even like going to the movies. My preference is dancing and comedy shows. Once I found out who I was, I stopped settling for those sweet talkers. I say thank you when they give their compliments and keep it moving.

Age eighteen does not make an individual an adult, even though society says it does. What makes you an adult is knowing who you are and knowing the direction your heading in. When your mind is set on that direction it will be worth everything that you had to go through to get there. However, if you settle for less you may end up living a life you really do not want. It is best to find out who you really are and what you really want to accomplish.

ACTION STEP:

Write out what you want within the next year. This will help you focus in that particular area. If anything comes your way that does not lead in that direction don't go that way. Remember at the end it will be worth it.

_____
_____
_____
_____
_____
_____
_____
_____
_____
_____
_____
_____
_____
_____
_____
_____
_____

LESSON NUMBER TWENTY-EIGHT

"GET CLARITY"

Your strength comes from knowing what you want. Once you **"GET CLARITY,"** there, you can see the end. Have you ever tried to open a jar, but the lid was to tight? Do you think it was because you were weak or because the lid was too tight? There is no right or wrong answer in this scenario. The point is you could not get the jar open, so you found someone who could. Why? Why did you go to the extent to ask someone to open the jar? I tell you why. You knew that you wanted what was inside even if it meant asking someone for help. You had clarity of what you wanted, and you got it.

Sometimes in our life there are going to be moments where we will have to pause and really think about what we want to do and how we are going to get it. It happens sometimes when a shift is happening in our life to where we have to choose a different direction. You have the same mission, but a different direction. To get even clearer you might have to ask for help on the journey. I know people who struggle in the area of asking for help when it comes to their work because they think it will make them look unsmart. This is a big deal! If you know what you want out of the jar and you're not afraid to ask, why not ask when it come to your work? Your mission is to get closer each day to your goal. When you find yourself stuck ask for help from a reliable source. Do not be afraid of someone telling you "no." Be on mission to not remain in the same place.

When I first went into a college I went to sign up for continuing education class. Next thing I know I signed up for college courses. I was a novice to applying for college. I never done it before. When I went to the desk I really was not sure if I used the proper language to get what I wanted, because I was not clear on what I wanted. I just knew I wanted more education. I did not realize I signed up for actually college course until I told my sister, who was attending college at the time, what I had done. If I would have shared with my sister what I was trying to do before I applied, the process could have gone much smoother.

Pride is when we do not want to show our weaker side. Getting clarity is essential to your next level. I share my experience of real-life situations so that you can see that I have many valuable learning lessons that could be helpful for you in life. You will be able to recognize when it is time to use the experience from a lesson when the time comes in your life. Recognize the direction you are going in then, if you need help along the way do not be ashamed to ask for what you need.

"GET CLARITY"

ACTION STEP:

Can you name a time when you were frustrated because you could not figure out the answer? How did the answer get solved? What can you do next time you feel stuck? Write your answer below.

LESSON TWENTY-NINE

"GET COMMITTED"

Do you want to sink or swim? It all depends on what you spend the most time thinking about. This lesson is for you to know that you won't sink once you "Get Committed!" You get committed by starving your distractions and feeding your focus. Commitment takes a lot of focus. IT takes a lot of guts to focus only on the task at hand. The reason why it takes guts is because other people may be going out having fun, but you have to have the discipline to remain committed to completion.

I made the outline for this book in December. The whole outline came to me in one sitting. Then in March I wrote until completion. I took a whole week off from work to focus on this book. I saw an opportunity to reach the youth in a mighty way so that they could skip going through the expereience themselves and instead learn from someone else's lessons. During this month of March there were obstacles that took place, but I moved past them all. The car accident happened which afterwards I took a four-day break. Then a few days later my city was on lockdown. However, I knew the benefits of you reading this book. I wanted to keep my commitment to myself to complete this book encouraging you so you can have the victory. I believe willingness to commit no matter what happens

"GET COMMITTED"

on the outside, is the real Victory!

My experience has taught me to swim through hard positions despite how it may look. Believing that there is a better story that could come from my life. This is where mental toughness plays a huge part. However, once you have had one Victory, you can go through the other storms of life much easier because you know what to do. I am a visual learner. One time I searched how to study on YouTube. I found someone who showed me how to take notes. This was a big deal for me. Unlike some of you, I was never taught how to take copious notes. Learning how to take notes help me so much more that I was willing to take better notes so that I could study them at home. I was committed to getting better so that I could pass my test. Even now, developing new skills in business, taking notes is a huge part of my daily life.

The question you should ask is, what are you willing to give? What type of person are you committed to becoming? In order for change to occur you have to be the change. We should evolve from day today or we will repeat the same thing of our yesterday. Getting committed allows us to position ourselves to the change we seek for ourselves. It means doing the hard stuff even if the outside situation is horrible. When you have clarity on the direction your heading, you can choose to commit to the change you want to see or remain the same.

ACTION STEPS:

IF this lesson sounded good I would like for you to stop reading and clap your hands five times.

Now write down how did it make you feel clapping your hands. The whole point is to see if you were willing to put the action steps in of clapping of your hands. You have to be committed to your process to make all the things you dreamed of work no matter how silly it sounds to someone else!

_____

_____

_____

_____

_____

_____

_____

_____

_____

_____

_____

_____

_____

_____

LESSON NUMBER THIRTY

"GET CONFIDENT"

We are finally here. Once you complete anything whether it's an assignment or getting your diploma it feels great doesn't it? I think my first thought is wow it's over. In the moment that you are celebrated it gives you a sense of joy, peace, and relief. It is done. It is completed. This brings on unstoppable confidence! I encourage you to **"GET CONFIDENT!"**

Hold on to the fact that you are uniquely you. Also hold on to the fact that your life experiences are not new! Just because it is new to you does not mean that no other being has faced what you have faced. Confidence breeds more great work. With great works, there will come some failures. Even the greatest basketball players miss shots. As you get back up from the failure do not let it be your focus. Your focus is always the end result and when that gets fuzzy, look at your last accomplishment!

Have you ever notice that when your confident, nothing can stop you. When my youngest son Leslie Jr. came home from taking his fifth-grade star test, I asked, him "How do you think you did?" He shared with me his grade in Math, Writing, and Reading. I looked at him knowing that in his mind he was sure of what he was saying. He had his predictions before his test results came back and he was pretty accurate. He mastered his math test with missing one answer. He let me know that there were a couple of questions on his reading test that he had trouble with. He said he was going to get a B and when the test came back he had a B. He was so sure of himself and made accurate predictions.

Life has its moments, but you can make it through. Believe in yourself no matter how hard it gets. Imagine you were getting into an Uber or Lyft car, and you ask the driver if they have enough gas to make it to your destination. Their response is "I think so." How confident are you in the driver getting you where you need to go? Your probably at a zero percent that they cannot complete the task. Look at your goals for the year? How confident are you completing the goal? Can you make your predictions right now?

Let the confidence of knowing you already have the victory light a spark within you to be clearer, more committed and more confidence. Confident people walk, talk, and act as if they know exactly where they are going. You may not have all the answers but stay in your lane of confidence! Do not look at the other people! Look in the mirror and remember YOU GOT THIS!

"GET CONFIDENT"

ACTION STEPS:

On a scale of one to ten with ten being the highest, how confident are you? How can you raise that number higher? Write your answer below.

VICTORIOUS CONTRACT

I am a Winner! A winner does winner things to get to their goals! Winners allow their higher self to guide them. A winner is confident in the in the direction they are going. A winner knows she/he is a champion and they walk, talk and act like a champion everyday! A winner stands in victory, because they play the game every day!

I _____, has chosen on this date_____, to play the game of life every single day! Winning equals Victory and in order for me to win, I will play the game!

The Victory Game!

Made in the USA
Middletown, DE
21 July 2024

57423021R00060